HOW TO
DESIGN
SURVEYS

THE SURVEY KIT

Purpose. The purposes of this 9-volume Kit are to enable readers to prepare and conduct surveys and become better users of survey results. Surveys are conducted to collect information by asking questions of people on the telephone, face-to-face, and by mail. The questions can be about attitudes, beliefs, and behavior as well as socioeconomic and health status. To do a good survey also means knowing how to ask questions, design the survey (research) project, sample respondents, collect reliable and valid information, and analyze and report the results. You also need to know how to plan and budget for your survey.

Users. The Kit is for students in undergraduate and graduate classes in the social and health sciences and for individuals in the public and private sectors who are responsible for conducting and using surveys. Its primary goal is to enable users to prepare surveys and collect data that are accurate and useful for primarily practical purposes. Sometimes, these practical purposes overlap the objectives of scientific research, and so survey researchers will also find the Kit useful.

Format of the Kit. All books in the series contain instructional objectives, exercises and answers, examples of surveys in use and illustrations of survey questions, guidelines for action, checklists of do's and don'ts, and annotated references.

Volumes in the Survey Kit:

1. **The Survey Handbook**
   Arlene Fink

2. **How to Ask Survey Questions**
   Arlene Fink

3. **How to Conduct Self-Administered and Mail Surveys**
   Linda B. Bourque and *Eve P. Fielder*

4. **How to Conduct Interviews by Telephone and in Person**
   James H. Frey and *Sabine Mertens Oishi*

5. **How to Design Surveys**
   Arlene Fink

6. **How to Sample in Surveys**
   Arlene Fink

7. **How to Measure Survey Reliability and Validity**
   Mark S. Litwin

8. **How to Analyze Survey Data**
   Arlene Fink

9. **How to Report on Surveys**
   Arlene Fink

THE SURVEY KIT
TSK✓5

HOW TO DESIGN SURVEYS

ARLENE FINK

SAGE Publications
International Educational and Professional Publisher
Thousand Oaks   London   New Delhi

For information address:

SAGE Publications, Inc.
2455 Teller Road
Thousand Oaks, California 91320
E-mail: order@sagepub.com

SAGE Publications Ltd.
6 Bonhill Street
London EC2A 4PU
United Kingdom

SAGE Publications India Pvt. Ltd.
M-32 Market
Greater Kailash I
New Delhi 110 048 India

Printed in the United States of America

Library of Congress Cataloging-in-Publication Data

Main entry under title:

The survey kit.
    p. cm.
    Includes bibliographical references.
    Contents: v. 1. The survey handbook / Arlene Fink — v. 2. How to ask survey questions / Arlene Fink — v. 3. How to conduct self-administered and mail surveys / Linda B. Bourque, Eve P. Fielder — v. 4. How to conduct interviews by telephone and in person / James H. Frey, Sabine Mertens Oishi — v. 5. How to design surveys / Arlene Fink — v. 6. How to sample in surveys / Arlene Fink — v. 7. How to measure survey reliability and validity / Mark S. Litwin — v. 8. How to analyze survey data / Arlene Fink — v. 9. How to report on surveys / Arlene Fink.
    ISBN 0-8039-7388-8 (pbk. : The survey kit : alk. paper)
    1. Social surveys. 2. Health surveys. I. Fink, Arlene.
HN29.S724   1995
300'.723—dc20   95-12712

This book is printed on acid-free paper.

95 96 97 98 99 10 9 8 7 6 5 4 3 2 1

Sage Production Editor: Diane S. Foster
Sage Copy Editor: Joyce Kuhn
Sage Typesetter: Janelle LeMaster

Contents

How to Design Surveys:
Learning Objectives

The aim of this book is to guide the reader in selecting and using appropriate survey designs. The following specific objectives are stated in terms of aspirations for the reader.

- Describe the major features of high-quality survey systems

- Identify the questions that structure survey designs

- Distinguish between experimental and observational designs

- Explain the characteristics, benefits, and concerns of these designs:

  - Concurrent controls with random assignment
  - Concurrent controls without random assignment
  - Self-controls
  - Historical controls
  - Cross-sectional designs
  - Cohort designs
  - Case-control designs

- Identify the risks to a design's internal validity

- Identify the risks to a design's external validity

1 Useful Surveys

Surveys are systems for collecting information on a broad range of subjects of interest in fields as diverse as education, sociology, demography, health, psychology, economics, business, and law. The best survey information systems have these six features:

- Specific, measurable objectives
- Sound research design
- Sound choice of population or sample
- Reliable and valid instruments
- Appropriate analysis
- Accurate reporting of survey results

1

MEASURABLE SURVEY OBJECTIVES

A survey's objectives are measurable if two or more people can easily agree on all the words and terms used to describe its purposes. Measurable survey objectives are illustrated in Example 1.1.

EXAMPLE 1.1
Three Measurable Objectives

Objective 1: To determine the quality of UCLA's education in preparing students with important job-related skills. Quality is a combination of the skill's importance and the value of UCLA's education in teaching the skill.

> *Comment:* This objective becomes measurable by clarifying the term *quality* to mean importance and value. You can infer that some of the survey's questions will take forms like "Select the top three most important skills" and "Rate how valuable UCLA's education is, using a scale on which 1 = not very valuable, 3 = medium value, and 5 = extremely valuable."

Objective 2: To determine changes from 1984 to 1992 qualifications, such as advanced placement units, among entering students.

> *Comment:* Qualifications are made measurable by "advanced placement units."

Objective 3: To compare the effectiveness of three approaches to continuing mental health education in a workshop setting. The three approaches are (a) traditional lecture and small group dis-

---

cussion, (b) computerized cases and small group discussion, and (c) computerized cases and self-instruction. An effective approach is one that encourages participants to appropriately resolve important (as defined by experts) patient care issues in practice.

> *Comment:* The effectiveness of an approach is defined to mean one that encourages workshop participants to appropriately resolve important patient care issues.

SOUND SURVEY DESIGN

A design is a way of arranging the environment in which a survey takes place. The environment consists of the individuals or groups of people, places, activities, or objects that are to be surveyed.

Some designs are relatively simple. A fairly uncomplicated survey might consist of a 10-minute interview on Wednesday with a group of 50 children to find out if they enjoyed a given film, and if so, why. This survey provides a cross-sectional portrait of one group's opinions at a particular time, and its design is called cross-sectional.

More complicated survey designs use environmental arrangements that are experiments, relying on two or more groups of participants or observations. When the views of randomly constituted groups of 50 children each are compared, for example, the survey design is experimental.

SOUND SURVEY SAMPLING

The participants in a survey may consist of all members of a given group, say, all 500 students in a school or all 70 patients who in the past 6 months have been diagnosed with diabetes. A subset of the population, say, 100 students and 25 patients, is a sample. The ideal sample has the same distribution of characteristics as the population. It has the same proportion of males and females, for example. To get a "representative" sample means using an unbiased method to choose survey participants, obtaining adequate numbers of participants, and collecting high-quality data by relying on valid and reliable survey instruments.

RELIABLE AND VALID SURVEY INSTRUMENTS

A reliable instrument is consistent; a valid one is accurate. Traditionally, survey instruments have been equated with mailed or self-administered questionnaires and telephone or face-to-face interviews. But the techniques for collecting and recording reliable and valid information perfected by survey researchers for these instruments also have been applied to other information-gathering techniques. These include forms for surveying the quality of medical care, the use of financial resources, and the content of the professional literature in business, health, and education.

One indication of the adaptation of these survey techniques to other instruments is the similarity of their purposes: to describe, compare, and predict. Another indication is how similar a questionnaire or interview form looks to, say, a record review form. Instead of asking questions of people, the questions are "asked" of records. As can be seen in the following examples, the two look identical:

Question from a self-administered questionnaire:

Which best describes your personal income last year? Circle *one* choice only.	
$25,000 or less	1
$25,001 - $40,000	2
$40,001 - $75,000	3
$75,001 or more	4

Question from a form for reviewing financial records:

Which best describes this person's income last year? Circle *one* choice only.	
$25,000 or less	1
$25,001 - $40,000	2
$40,001 - $75,000	3
$75,001 or more	4

All surveys, regardless of format, should only contain questions or items that are pertinent to the survey's objectives. The aim is to produce reliable and valid data. Reliable data are the results of consistent responses over time and between and among observers and respondents. Valid data come from surveys that measure what they purport to measure.

APPROPRIATE SURVEY ANALYSIS

Surveys use conventional statistical and other scholarly methods to analyze findings. The choice of method depends on whether the survey aims for description, comparison, association or correlation, or prediction, and also the size of the sample. The analysis must account also for the type of survey data available: nominal (categorical), ordinal, or numerical. Nominal or categorical data come from scales that have no numerical value such as gender and race. Ordinal data come from rating scales and may range, say, from most favored to least favored or from strongly agree to strongly disagree. Numerical data come from measures that ask for numbers like age, years living at present address, and height.

ACCURATE SURVEY REPORTS

Fair and accurate reporting means staying within the boundaries set by the survey's design, sampling methods, data collection quality, and choice of analysis. Accurate survey reports require knowledge of how to use tables and figures to present information.

Survey Design:
The Arranged Environment

To be useful and valid, surveys should be conducted in an arranged or designed environment. Consider these illustrations in Example 1.2.

EXAMPLE 1.2
Illustrative Survey Designs

Survey 1: College Students and Graduates

Background: Each year, UCLA prepares a student profile. Data for the profile come from records (including those maintained by the financial aid office and student loan services) and mailed student questionnaires.

Objective: To determine the quality of UCLA's education in preparing students with important job-related skills

Instrument: Self-administered questionnaire. Students were asked to indicate on a 3-point scale how important each of eight items was in preparing them for their job and then to rate on a 4-point scale the quality of UCLA's preparation in each of the eight areas.

Design: Descriptive (or observational), specifically, cross-sectional

Results: The responses for graduates who were employed full-time and not enrolled in graduate school are summarized in Figure 1.1.

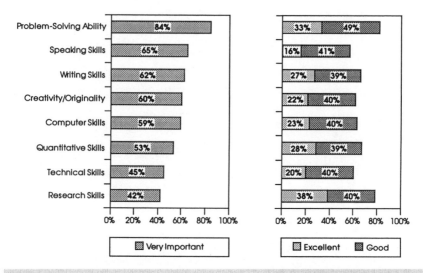

NOTE: Students were asked to indicate on a 3-point scale how important each of the eight items were in preparing them for their job and then to rate on a four-point scale the quality of UCLA's preparation in each of the eight areas. The responses for graduates who were employed full-time and not enrolled in graduate school are summarized in the chart above. *Problem-solving ability* was the skill most often considered by respondents to be very important for the work they were currently doing and it also received the highest combined rating of excellent or good. *Speaking skills* were second in terms of those who considered them very important for their job but last in the combined rating of excellent or good.

Figure 1-1 UCLA Preparation

Interpretation: Problem-solving ability was the skill most often considered by respondents to be very important for the work they were currently doing, and it also received the highest combined rating of excellent or good. Speaking skills were second in terms of those who considered them very important for their job but last in the combined rating of excellent or good.

Comment: This survey provides a cross section of descriptive information at one point in time. The survey collected its information directly from students by using a self-administered questionnaire.

Survey 2: Entering Students

Background: As part of its annual student profile, UCLA collects data on students who enter with advanced placement (AP) units.

Objective: To assess the extent of change in the proportion of students entering UCLA with AP credits

Instrument: Standardized record review (records from Undergraduate Admissions and Relations With Schools)

Design: Cross-sectional (to study trends)

Results: Figure 1.2 shows the percentages of entering students with AP credits in 1984 and 1992.

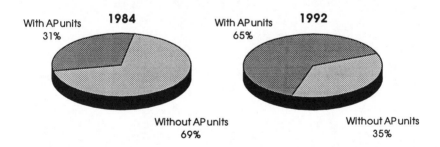

NOTE: The percentage of students entering with AP units has continued to increase from 31% in 1984 to 65% in 1992, and the average amount of college credit earned increased from 14 to 18 units.

Figure 1-2 First-Year Students Enter With One Quarter's College Credit

Interpretation: The percentage of students entering with AP units increased from 31% in 1984 to 65% in 1992. The average amount of college credit earned increased from 14 to 18 points.

Comment: The survey provided a description of trends in accumulating AP credits of two entering classes. Data came from surveying records, using the same form each time.

Survey 3: Comparing Educational Approaches

Background: The city is conducting a study to identify an effective approach to continuing education in mental health.

Purpose: To compare the effectiveness of three approaches to instruction in a workshop setting

Instrument: Self-administered questionnaires and standardized 10-item observation form used by two trained observers monitoring each workshop

Design: An experiment with concurrent controls in which survey participants are **not** randomly assigned to groups. Here, 200 eligible community mental health workers are assigned to three workshops, depending on their preference. The first workshop (Group 1) uses traditional lecture and small group discussion, the second (Group 2) relies on computerized cases and small group discussion, and the third (Group 3) employs computerized cases and self-instruction. Observations are made during each workshop session. Participants complete a questionnaire at the conclusion of the 3-hour workshop.

Results: Agreement between the two observers in each workshop was 81%, 76%, and 93% in Groups 1, 2, and 3, respectively. No differences were found in preference for type of instruction among participants in the three groups. Participants in the computerized cases and self-instruction group (Group 3) rated their experiences as "likely to carry over into their work" significantly more often than did the other two groups ($p < .05$.).

Interpretation: Participants in the computerized cases and self-instruction group stated that their learning is likely to carry over to their jobs significantly more often than the other groups stated. Their belief should now be tested in a controlled study.

Comment: This experimental study used a traditional survey method (a self-administered questionnaire) and an applied survey method (standardized observation) to collect data. Each type of survey information was collected just once: during the workshop (the observations) and at the conclusion of workshop participation (the questionnaire).

Survey 4: Comparing Educational Approaches

Background: The city is conducting a study to identify an effective approach to continuing education in mental health.

Purpose: To compare the effectiveness of three approaches to instruction by determining the number of important issues per topic (e.g., technical care, doctor-patient relationship, coordination of care) addressed in practice by participants. Important issues in patient care have been identified by a panel of experts.

Instrument: Self-administered questionnaires and case record review

Design: An experiment with concurrent controls in which survey participants are randomly assigned to groups. Here, 200 eligible community mental health workers are assigned at random to three workshops. The first workshop (Group 1) uses traditional lecture and small group discussion, the second (Group 2) relies on computerized cases and small group discussion, and the third (Group 3) employs computerized cases and self-instruction. Participants complete a questionnaire at the conclusion of the 3-hour workshop. Before participation and 6 months after, the case records of participants are reviewed, and the number of important issues addressed is counted.

Results: The number of issues (e.g., improving the doctor-patient relationship, fostering patient responsibility) addressed did not differ among the groups at baseline but differed significantly after the intervention. The number dropped significantly in Group 1 (2 to 0.5, $p < .05$); rose, but not significantly, in Group 2 (0.5 to 1.5, *ns*, or not significant), and increased substantially and significantly in Group 3 (1 to 3.75, $p < .05$). [More information on testing statistical significance and p values is given in **How to Analyze Survey Data**, Vol. 8 in this series.] These results are shown in Figure 1.3.

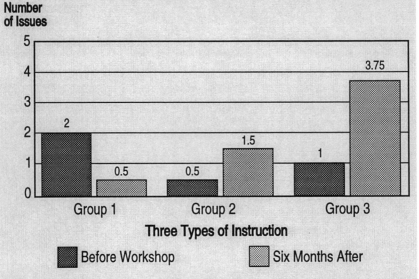

Figure 1-3   Number of Issues Per Topic Before and After Workshop

When Group 3 participants were asked to rate the likelihood that participation in the workshop contributed to their knowledge of important issues in caring for patients' mental health needs, nearly all (98%) chose ratings of 4 ("probably") or 5 ("definitely likely").

Interpretation: Computerized cases and self-instruction are an effective approach to continuing education for the city's mental health workers.

Comment: This study is experimental and randomly assigns participants to one of three groups. It uses questionnaires and record reviews to collect data.

The aim of Survey 1 is to find out if UCLA has done a good job in preparing its students with important job-related skills. The design used provides a one-time-only portrait of students' opinions as gathered from a self-administered questionnaire. The design is called cross-sectional and is discussed in much greater detail in Chapter 2. Survey 2 collects data from records in two cross-sectional studies.

Survey 3 uses an experimental design to compare the results of observations and self-administered questionnaires. Experimental designs involve arranging the environment so that comparisons can be made. A relatively simple experimental design, for example, would compare the reading ability of children who have participated in an innovative program with the reading ability of children who have not participated. Survey 4 also uses an experimental design, but in this case the three groups have been randomly assembled. Surveys 3 and 4 use self-administered questionnaires. Survey 3 also uses observations; Survey 4 also uses record reviews.

The four surveys use typical survey designs. These can be grouped into two general types: descriptive (also called observational) and experimental. How do you choose? Answer the following questions to select the right design.

Checklist of Questions to Ask
in Choosing a Survey Design

✓ **What is the survey's aim—describe, compare, predict?**

Surveys produce information to describe, compare, and predict attitudes, opinions, values, and behavior based on what people say or see and what is contained in records about them and their activities. Example 1.3 illustrates the three major survey aims.

EXAMPLE 1.3
Describing, Comparing, or Predicting

Describing

Objective: To *describe* the quality of life of men over and under 65 years of age with different health characteristics (e.g., the presence or absence of common conditions like hypertension and diabetes) and social characteristics (e.g., living alone or living with someone; employed or not), all of whom have had surgery within the past 2 years for prostate cancer

Target: Men of differing ages, health, and social characteristics who have had surgery for prostate cancer within the past 2 years

Number of times surveyed: Once, within 2 years of surgery

Comparing—Design 1

Objective: At the end of the school year, to *compare* a sample of boys and girls in Grades 1 through 6 in five schools regarding their views on their school's new dress code

Target: Boys and girls in Grades 1 through 6 in five elementary schools

Number of times surveyed: Once, at the end of the school year

Comparing—Design 2

Objective: Before and after participation in a safety course, to *compare* parents of children under 5 years of age, between 6 and 12, and 13 and over in terms of their opinions of their ability to cope with potential accidents and injuries in the home

Target: Parents who participate in a safety course

Number of times surveyed: Twice, before and after participation

Comparing—Design 3

Objective: To *compare* a sample of employees in three companies annually for 3 years about their views on uncompensated leave time

Target: Employees in three companies

Number of times surveyed: Three times, once each year

Predicting

Objective: In 1994 and 1995, to determine the extent to which gender, education or income *predicts* preferences for differing leisure activities, including reading, sports, movies, and travel

Target: Male and female high school graduates, each of whom earns an annual income of less than $30,000, between $30,000 and $60,000, or more than $60,000

Number of times surveyed: Twice, in 1994 and in 1995

✓ Is a control group included?

The term "group" refers to an assembly of people, institutions, or units that is defined by participation in a program or intervention or by shared personal, social, or health characteristics. Three illustrative groups are people who receive an experimental medicine, employees who implement the terms of a flexible work-hours policy for the first time, and schools that try out an innovative adult literacy program. When a group takes part in an untested intervention, such as those just mentioned, it is called the **experimental** group. The experimental group is contrasted with the **control** group, which does not participate in the experiment or innovation.

A basic survey design compares experimental and control groups that have been created just for the survey. For example, you can survey people trying out a new medicine (the experimental group) with a group of people using a traditional medicine (the control group) and also with a second group not taking any medicine (a second control group). Sometimes one group serves as its own control. For example, you can survey people just before they take a new medicine and again 1 year later. These two designs are **prospective** because the events of interest occur after the study begins. That is, the study begins and then the effects of the new medicine on people are surveyed over time, or **longitudinally.**

Another example of a longitudinal, prospective survey involves identifying a group whose members share important characteristics (e.g., severe headaches) and then surveying some or all of the members of the group at least once more. This group, called a **cohort,** can also be compared to a control group.

Retrospective designs are those for which the events have already occurred. For example, teens between 13 and 17 years of age who get headaches at least once a month and teens of the same age who rarely get headaches can be interviewed and the results compared. The teens with the headaches are called the **cases** and the teens without constitute the control group. This design is retrospective because the headaches were present before the study was initiated. A useful way to distinguish between prospective and retrospective designs is to focus on the direction of inquiry. If the direction is forward, the design is prospective. If the inquiry follows a path backward through time, the design is retrospective.

✓ Who is eligible?

The eligibility criteria separate those who are eligible for participation in the survey from those who are not. Those who are eligible are the target of the survey. The survey's findings can be applied only to the target.

In Example 1.3 under Describing, the target of the survey's findings is men of differing ages, health, and social characteristics who have had surgery for prostrate cancer within the past 2 years. Men who have had chemotherapy or observational treatment or who have had surgery more than 2 years ago are not eligible for inclusion in the survey. Because they are not eligible, the survey's findings about quality of life may not be applicable to these men. A survey's findings are only applicable or **generalizable** to the eligible participants—assuming they participate—because eligible nonparticipants may differ from participants. Nonparticipants' views are likely not as strong, for example; the survey results may only or primarily be based on the views of advocates.

In Example 1.3 under Comparing (Design 1), the target is schoolchildren in Grades 1 through 6. These children are the only ones who are eligible for the survey. Those in kindergarten or Grade 7 are not the target, and the findings may not apply to them.

The criteria for inclusion in a survey come from two sources: the survey's target population and geographic and temporal proximity. Consider the illustrative inclusion criteria in Example 1.4.

EXAMPLE 1.4
Illustrative Inclusion Criteria:
Target Population, Geography, and Time

Target Population

For a survey of quality of life after prostate cancer surgery:
- Men who have had surgery
- Men over the age of 65 years

For a survey of young children's attitudes toward school:
- Children in Grades 1 through 6

Geographic Proximity

For a survey of quality of life after prostate cancer surgery:
- Must live within 30 miles of the Survey Center

For a survey of young children's attitudes toward school:
- Must attend one of five elementary schools in the district

Temporal Proximity

For a survey of quality of life after prostate cancer surgery:
- Must have had surgery within the past 2 years

For a survey of young children's attitudes toward school:
- Must have participated in one of two current experimental reading programs

Practical inclusion criteria are often set simply to conserve resources. If the survey's participants live close by, then the costs of travel to and from face-to-face interviews is less than if relatively long distances must be crossed. Local calls (for telephone interviews) cost less than long-distance calls. Choosing sites with potentially large numbers of eligible respondents can simplify the logistics of the survey: Instead of surveying participants in many sites, surveys can be administered in relatively few.

Surveys sometimes have exclusion criteria. These are special criteria that apply to potential respondents whose inclusion is likely to impair the actual functioning of the survey or skew its data. Consider some exclusion criteria presented in Example 1.5.

EXAMPLE 1.5
Illustrative Exclusion Criteria

- Not likely to complete the survey (including people with memory deficits, major psychiatric illness, or severe vision impairment for written surveys and hearing impairment for interviews)

- Unable to read, understand, or write the language of the survey

- An event that happens rarely (e.g., infrequent occurrences of a social, educational, or medical event)

- The presence of only some of the inclusion criteria (e.g., a person is the right age and lives in the geographic area being surveyed but is unable to read English)

2 Classification of Designs for Surveys

Surveys are systems for collecting information to describe, compare, and predict attitudes, opinions, values, knowledge, and behavior. An essential component of the system is the design or environmental arrangement in which data are collected, analyzed, and interpreted. Designs can be categorized as experimental or descriptive (sometimes called observational), as depicted below.

■ Experimental

Experimental designs are characterized by arranging to compare two or more groups, at least one of which is experimental. The other is a control (or comparison) group. An experimental group is given a new or untested, innovative program, intervention, or treatment. The control is given an alternative. A group is any collective unit. Sometimes, the unit is made up of individuals with a common experience, such as men who have had surgery, children who are in a reading program, or victims of violence. At other times, the unit is naturally occurring: a classroom, business, or hospital.

Concurrent controls in which participants are randomly assigned to groups. **Concurrent** means that each group is assembled at the same time. For example, when 10 of 20 schools are randomly assigned to an experimental group while, at the same time, 10 are assigned to a control, you have a randomized controlled trial or true experiment.

Concurrent controls in which participants are not randomly assigned to groups. These are called nonrandomized controlled trials, quasi-experiments, or nonequivalent controls.

Self-controls. These require premeasures and postmeasures and are called longitudinal or before-after designs.

Historical controls. These make use of data collected for participants in other surveys.

Combinations. These can consist of concurrent controls with or without pre- and postmeasures.

■ Descriptive (Observational)

Descriptive designs produce information on groups and phenomena that already exist. No new groups are created. Descriptive designs are also called observational by some surveyors.

Cross sections. These provide descriptive data at one fixed point in time. A survey of American voters' current choices is a cross-sectional survey.

Cohorts. These forward-looking designs provide data about changes in a specific population. Suppose a survey of the aspirations of athletes participating in the 1996 Olympics is given in 1996, 2000, and 2004. This is a cohort design, and the cohort is 1996 Olympians.

Case controls. These retrospective studies go back in time to help explain a current phenomenon. At least two groups are included. When first you survey the medical records of a sample of smokers and nonsmokers of the same age, health, and socioeconomic status and then compare the findings, you have used a case-control design.

Experiments

Surveys in experimental studies can be conducted any number of times before, during, and after a program or intervention. Surveys conducted beforehand serve many important purposes—for example, to select groups to participate in a program, check the support for a program, ensure comparability of groups, and provide a basis for monitoring change. The uses of surveys as premeasures are illustrated in Example 2.1.

EXAMPLE 2.1
Surveys as Premeasures

To Select Participants

A self-administered questionnaire was given to all parents. They were asked to specify the number of years of formal education they had completed in this or any other country. They were also asked to rate whether they would be willing to participate in one of two experimental programs to improve literacy. All parents who stated that they had completed fewer than 10 years of schooling and indicated that they were definitely willing were eligible to participate in the program.

To Check the Support for a Program

A mailed questionnaire is sent to all residents to find out if they will participate in a program to teach home-based injury prevention. The questionnaire asks residents if they are willing to be in a control group, if randomly selected.

To Ensure Comparability of Groups

Students are assigned to the experimental and control groups. A survey is made to compare ages and reading levels before the start of the experiment to check that the two groups are similar with respect to these two important variables.

To Provide a Basis for Monitoring Change

Prisoners who have been selected to participate in either the experimental group or the control group are interviewed using a standardized measure of rage. A similar survey will be given after the experimental group completes 6 months of an art therapy program.

Surveys can also begin during an intervention to measure change and after to measure the outcomes and impact of programs and interventions. These uses are illustrated in Example 2.2.

EXAMPLE 2.2
Surveys as Interim and Postmeasures

To Measure Change

People over 65 years of age who have been to the emergency room for a fall are interviewed within 2 weeks and then 3, 6, and 12 months later. The experimental group has received a geriatric assessment; the control group has not. The interviews are used to compare the two groups with respect to their social, psychological, and physical functioning.

To Measure Outcomes

Prisoners in an art therapy program are interviewed by two psychiatrists within 3 months of completing their course of study. The results are compared with those obtained from interviews with the control group.

To Measure Impact

Elderly people receiving and not receiving special geriatric assessments after a fall are surveyed 1, 3, and 5 years later. The purpose of the surveys at 3 and 5 years is to assess and compare impact over time.

CONCURRENT CONTROLS
AND RANDOM ASSIGNMENT

The groups in this design are created by first setting up eligibility criteria and then randomly assigning eligible "units" to one or more experimental and control groups. The groups can be observed and measured periodically. If the experimental group is observed to differ from the control group in a positive way on important outcome variables (e.g., satisfaction, quality of life, health, and knowledge), the experiment is considered successful within certain predefined limits. The units that are randomly assigned may be individuals (e.g., Persons A, B, C, etc. or Teachers A, B, C, etc.) or clusters of individuals (e.g., schools, residential blocks, hospitals).

Random assignment (sometimes called randomization or random allocation) means that individuals or clusters of individuals are assigned by chance to the experimental group or the control group. With random assignment, the occurrence of previous events has no value in predicting future events. The alternative to randomization is regulation of the allocation process so that you can predict group assignment, such as assigning people admitted to a hospital on odd days of the month to the experimental group and those admitted on even days to the control group.

Example 2.3 shows one method of randomly assigning units to an experimental group and control group. The example makes use of a table of random numbers. Tables like these are available in most standard statistics texts. Random numbers can also be generated by computer; the principles underlying the use of a table or list of numbers are the same.

EXAMPLE 2.3
Using a Table of Random Numbers
in Random Assignment to Groups

Twenty schools are eligible to participate in a trial of a program to improve public speaking skills. Ten are to be in the experimental group and 10 in the control group. If the experimental program is more effective in improving skills and confidence, it will be offered to the control schools free of charge.

The names of all 20 schools are placed on a list and assigned a number from 1 to 20 (e.g., John Adams School = 1; Robert Burns School = 2; Joseph Zermatt School = 20). Then, using a table of random numbers, the first 10 numbers that appear are chosen for the experimental group. Here is how the selection is made.

1. *Randomly identify the row.* Place 10 slips of paper in a jar. Select a number. Place the slip back in the jar and make a second selection. Return the slip to the jar. Suppose the first number is 3 and the second is 5. Using the table below, and starting with the first column, this corresponds to the third block and the fifth row of that block, or number 1 4 5 7 5.

2. *Randomly identify the column.* Select two numbered slips from the jar. Suppose you get a 2 and a 1. Go to the second block of columns and the first column beginning with 1: 1 9 7 0 4.

---

3. *Choose the experimental group.* Follow down to where 1 4 5 7 5 and the column with 1 9 7 0 4 intersect at 3 5 4 9 0.

4. Ten schools are needed for the sample. You must therefore select 10 numbers between 01 and 20. Moving down column 2, and starting with the numbers below 3 5 4 9 0, the first double-digit number you come to is 70. The numbers you find that meet your needs from that point on are 12, 20, 09, 02, 01, 13, 18, 03, 04, and 16. These are the schools that constitute the experimental group.

18283	19704^2	45387	23476	12323	34865
46453	21547	39246	93198	98005	65988
19076	23453	32760	27166	75032	99945
36743	89563	12378	98223	23465	25408
22125	19786	23498	76575	76435	63442
76009	77099	43788	36659	74399	**03432**
09878	76549	88877	26587	44633	77659
34534	44475	56632	34350	**01768**	29027
83109	75899	34877	21357	24300	00869
89063	43555	32700	76497	36099	97956
				94656	34689
09887	67770	69975	54465	**13896**	**04645**
23280	34572	99443	98765	34978	42880
93856	23090	22257	67400	23580	24376
21256	50863	56934	70993	34765	30996
14575^1	35490^3	23645	22179	35788	37600
23276	70^{4}870	**20087**	66665	78876	58007
87530	45738	**09998**	45397	47500	34875
00791	32164	97665	27589	90087	**16004**
99003	32567	**02878**	38602	**18700**	23455
14367	64999	78453	40078	53727	28759

Explanations:

Numbers in **bold** = Sample of 10, consisting of numbers, between 01 and 20.

1 = Two random choices of numbers in a jar yield 1 (column) and 5 (block).

2 = Two random choices of numbers in a jar yield 2 (column) and 1 (row).

3 = Intersection of superscripts 1 and 2.

4 = Start here to get the sample.

Designs that use concurrent controls and random assignment are also called randomized trials, randomized controlled trials, and true experiments. Example 2.4 gives two illustrations of their use with random assignment of individuals and of groups or clusters of individuals.

EXAMPLE 2.4
Experimental Studies
With Concurrent Controls
and Random Assignment to Groups

1. Comparing Medical and Surgical Therapy

Medical and surgical therapy were compared for patients with stable ischemic heart disease. (Ischemia refers to an insufficient supply of blood to the heart.) Over 4 years, half of all eligible patients in each of 10 medical centers were assigned at random to either the medical group or the surgical therapy group. The design can be illustrated as follows:

Medical Center	Intervention	
	Surgical Therapy	Medical Therapy
1 (100 patients)	50	50
2 (60 patients)	30	30
3 (120 patients)	60	60
4 (90 patients)	45	45
5 (100 patients)	50	50

$\rightarrow$

	Intervention	
6 (90 patients)	45	45
7 (70 patients)	35	35
8 (150 patients)	75	75
9 (150 patients)	75	75
10 (100 patients)	50	50

To find out about length of survival, patients were compared across medical centers (e.g., patients in Medical Center 1 compared to 2, 3, and so on; those in Medical Center 2 compared to 3, 4, and so on). Comparisons were also made between patients in surgical versus medical therapy regardless of medical center.

No differences were found in survival between and across medical centers and type of therapy. The surgical group had a higher quality of life, as manifested by relief of chest pain, scores on a functional status questionnaire, and reduced need for drug therapy.

2. Changes in Physician Compliance
With Practice Guidelines

The investigators used a randomized controlled experimental design to measure changes in individual physician compliance with blood transfusion guidelines following an experimental education program.

Pairs of teaching and community hospitals were randomly selected from all hospitals who met entry criteria (including rates of transfusion for selected procedures and diagnoses) within three health service areas. After one teaching hospital and one community hospital had been randomly selected from the entire list, a second hospital of each type was randomly identified from one of the other two health service areas to minimize the risk of experimental contamination due to physicians' practicing at multiple sites within a health service area. One surgical service in each matched pair was then randomly assigned to the study group and the other to the control group; within each hospital the medical service was assigned to the treatment group opposite from surgery. To measure changes in physician practices, compliance with guidelines for transfusion were analyzed for control and study physicians for 6 months before and 6 months following the experimental intervention.

Random selection is different from random assignment. In the second illustration, hospitals are randomly selected from all that are eligible. In some surveys, the entire eligible population is used; in others, only a sample is chosen. In most instances, probability sampling methods (like random sampling) are preferred. Probability sampling methods are those in which all eligible units have a known chance of selection.

Experimental designs using randomly constituted concurrent controls enable you to pinpoint and isolate an intervention's outcomes. They are the gold standard or the preferred designs when doing scientific research. With a large enough sample, these designs can control nearly all errors or **biases** from extraneous factors, including those that you do not know about and do not measure. In fact, randomization helps ensure that all groups have, on average, the same distribution of extraneous factors if the sample is large enough.

What are these errors or biases that lead to false conclusions? One of the most potentially damaging biases comes from the method of "selection." Selection bias is present when people who are initially different from one another and have differing prior risks for the outcome of interest are compared. Suppose a survey is conducted after Schools A and B participate in a comparative test of two approaches to reading. The survey results reveal that children in School A's reading program—the control—score higher (better) on an attitude-to-reading inventory than do children in School B—the experiment. Although the results may suggest a failed experiment, the two groups may have been different to begin with, even if they appeared to be similar. For instance, both schools' children may be alike in socioeconomic background, reading ability, and the competence of their reading teachers, but they may differ in other important ways. School B, for example, may have a better library, a friendlier librarian, more resources to spend on extra program reading, a social system that reinforces reading, and so on. To avoid bias from the selection process, the survey team should have randomly assigned students into experimental and control groups regardless of school.

Biases can arise from unrecognized as well as recognized characteristics of the individuals compared. Randomization is the only known way to control for unknown biases and to distribute them fairly.

Designs using concurrent controls and random assignment are complex. One issue that often arises concerns the appropriate unit of randomization. Sometimes, for practical purposes, clusters (schools, companies) rather than individuals are chosen for random assignment. You cannot assume, however, that the individuals forming the groups are comparable in the same way as they would have been had they been randomized as individuals.

Other potential sources of bias include failure to adequately monitor the randomization process and to follow uniform procedures across all groups. Training people and monitoring the quality of the randomization process are essential.

In some randomized studies, the participants and investigators do not know which group is the experimental one and which is the control: This is the double-blind experiment. When participants do not know but investigators do, this is called the blinded trial. In many surveys, it is often logistically or ethically difficult to "blind" participants, and this may bias the results. One approach is to "blind" the persons administering the survey, as illustrated in Example 2.5.

EXAMPLE 2.5
"Blinding" in Experimental Designs

Two groups of employees have completed 4-week training courses to improve selected business skills. Employees were randomly assigned either to the regular course or to the experimental course. A major objective of the experimental course is the improvement of negotiation skills; this topic is not covered in the regular course. At the end of the 4 weeks, all employees are interviewed by specially trained examiners who rate the employees' skills in setting up contracts for the company. Each employee is rated by two examiners, neither of whom knows whether the employee has participated in the experimental course or the regular course.

To maximize the applicability or generalizability of the results, experiments should probably be conducted in many places with a variety of participants over a number of years.

The technical and financial resources needed for concurrently randomized controlled experiments are high, but the potential for sound conclusions justifies the costs. However, despite their scientific virtues, experimental designs with concurrent controls do not automatically fit all survey situations. The designs are not equipped to provide data for quick decision making. Sometimes, randomization is not ethical if a group is to be denied an experimental intervention that has a reasonable chance of having more benefits than risks. Finally, you cannot assume that randomization alone guarantees that your survey will produce "truth." At the minimum, valid survey findings depend on clearly stated purposes, justified samples, accurate data collection, and appropriate statistical analysis and interpretation.

Guidelines for Experimental Designs Involving Randomly Assigned Concurrent Controls

The following guidelines are recommended when using survey designs with concurrent controls and random assignment:

1. Define the target population.
2. Choose inclusion and exclusion criteria that are theoretically appropriate and practical.

3. If a sample of eligible participants is to be surveyed, use probability sampling (like random sampling) to select it.

4. Use a table of random numbers, computer-generated list, or other means to ensure that the experimental and control groups are randomly constituted.

5. Monitor the effects of potential errors from inadequate implementation of randomization, lack of uniform experimental and control programs, and discovery by participants that they are in the experimental (or control) group.

6. Decide in advance of the survey how you will handle the ethical implications of denying a potentially beneficial intervention to the control group.

7. Be certain that you have the resources to implement and monitor the logistics of a randomized trial or true experiment.

8. Do not rest after you have implemented the design: Check to see that the data collection and analysis methods are equally valid.

CONCURRENT CONTROLS BUT NO RANDOM ASSIGNMENT

Nonrandomized, concurrent controls (quasi-experimental designs) come about when you have at least two already existing groups, one of which is designated experimental (Example 2.6).

EXAMPLE 2.6
Concurrent Controls
but No Random Assignment

1. Studies have shown that children who move many times tend
   to miss more schooling and are more at risk for significant
   behavioral problems than are children with stable addresses.
   Teachers, counselors, and nurses in three schools participated
   in a program to teach them to survey children who have moved
   frequently. The purpose of the survey was to guide school and
   health professionals to anticipate potential problems and,
   when necessary, to make effective referrals. Two schools were
   chosen to act as controls. In the control schools, no special
   intervention was introduced. At the end of 3 years, children
   whose families met relocation criteria were surveyed in both
   sets of schools.

2. A nonrandomized trial was used to test a program to reduce
   the use of antipsychotic drugs in nursing homes. The program
   was based on behavioral techniques to manage behavior problems and encourage gradual antipsychotic drug withdrawal.
   Two rural community nursing homes with elevated antipsychotic use were in the experimental group, and two comparable
   homes were selected as concurrent controls. Residents in both
   groups of homes had comparable demographic characteristics
   and functional status, and each group had a baseline rate of
   29 days of antipsychotic use per 100 days of nursing home
   residence.

   Concurrent control designs without randomization are easier to implement than experimental designs with randomization. Perhaps their feasibility accounts for the fact that they
may be the oldest design, as illustrated in Example 2.7, taken
from the Bible (King James version), Daniel 1:11-15.

EXAMPLE 2.7
Concurrent Controls
Without Random Assignment
—The Book of Daniel—

Then Daniel said to Melzar, . . . Prove thy servants, I beseech thee, ten days; and let them give us pulse [seeds from peas and beans] to eat, and water to drink. Then let our countenances be looked upon before thee, and the countenance of the children that eat of the portion of the king's meat: and as thou seest, deal with thy servants.

So he consented to them in this matter, and proved them ten days. And at the end of ten days their countenances appeared fairer and fatter in flesh than all the children which did eat the portion of the king's meat. Thus Melzar took away the portion of their meat, and the wine that they should drink; and gave them pulse.

Random assignment is sometimes infeasible, as it would have been in the case of the "children" who ate the king's meat and those who ate pulse. As another example, suppose you wanted to survey prisoners who participated in a 3-year art therapy program. Each year, 10 prisoners in three facilities will participate in the program; three other facilities have agreed to serve as the control. The primary purpose of the program is to improve prisoners' ability to cope with potentially violent situations by using art as one outlet for emotions like rage and fear. By the end of the third year, 90 prisoners will have participated. In this example, random assignment would probably be logistically complicated and costly, and so you might look for an alternative design.

The use of nonrandomly selected controls, although relatively practical, increases the likelihood that external factors will bias a survey's results. A typical bias associated with nonrandom assignment is selection or membership bias.

Membership bias refers to characteristics that members of groups share simply because they are in the group. The idea is that preexisting groups are usually not assembled haphazardly: they come together precisely because they share similar values, attitudes, behavior, or social and health status. Examples of groups with shared characteristics are people who live in the same neighborhood (they are likely to be similar in their incomes), children who have the same teacher (they may share similar abilities), patients who see a particular physician (they may have a particular medical problem), prisoners at a minimum security facility (they have committed a certain level of crime), and prisoners at a maximum security facility (they also have committed a certain level of crime but it differs from that of prisoners in a minimum security facility). Only random assignment can guarantee that two groups are equivalent from the point of view of all variables that may influence a survey's outcomes.

Membership bias can seriously challenge a survey's accuracy. When you use concurrent controls without random assignment, you should administer a premeasure to determine the equivalence of the groups at the start or at **baseline** on potentially important characteristics. In Example 2.6, the second illustration does this by reporting that residents in each of the two homes had comparable demographic characteristics, functional status, and use of antipsychotics.

The comparability of groups at baseline is often discussed in a table. Example 2.8 shows how this is done. In the example, the characteristics of two concurrent, nonrandomly assigned groups are compared. The groups are participants in a program to teach parenting to young women.

EXAMPLE 2.8
Comparing Baseline
Characteristics in a Table

Characteristics	Experimental (*n* = 125)	Control (*n* = 147)
Infant gender, % male	40.0	42.0
Birthweight, ≤1,500 g, %	24.8	23.8
Maternal age, year, %[a]		
15 - 17	29.6	9.5
18 - 19	32.8	18.4
20 - 24	37.6	72.1
Frequent moving, %	24.8	23.8

a. $p < .001$ for those in the experimental compared with those in the control. (For more about the uses of p in tests of significance, see **How to Analyze Survey Data,** Vol. 8 in this series.)

You can see from the table that the participants in the program differ in their age. If age is an important factor for success in the program, the differences that preexist in the two groups pose a serious problem in this design. A variable that is more likely to be present in one group of subjects than in another or that is related to the outcome of interest and confuses or confounds the results is called a **confounding variable**.

Statistical methods, like analysis of covariance (ANCOVA) or the Mantel-Haenzel chi-square, are available to "control" for the influence of confounding variables when random assignment is not used. As a rule, however, it is better to control for confounders before collecting survey data—that is, as part of design and sampling—than afterward during analysis.

SELF-CONTROLS

A design with self-controls uses a group of participants to serve as its own comparison. Suppose, for example, students were surveyed three times: at the beginning of the year to find out their attitudes toward community service, immediately after their participation in a 1-year course to find out the extent to which their attitudes changed, and at the end of 2 years to ascertain if the change is sustained. This three-measurement strategy describes a design using the students as their own control. In the example, the survey measures the students once before and twice after the intervention (a new course). Designs of this type are also called before-and-after or pretest-posttest designs.

Self-controlled survey designs are prone to several biases. Participants may become excited about taking part in an experiment; they may mature physically, emotionally, and intellectually; or historical events can intervene. For example, suppose a survey reveals that the students in a 2-year test of a school-based intervention acquire important attitudes and behaviors and retain them over time. This desirable result may be due to the new course or to the characteristics of the students who, from the start, may have been motivated to learn and have become even more excited by being in an experimental program. Another possibility is that over the 2-year inter-vention period students may have matured intellectually, and this development, rather than the program, is responsible for the learning. Also, historical or external events may have occurred to cloud the effects of the new course. For example, suppose that during the year an inspired teacher gives several stimulating lectures to the students. The students' outstand-ing performance on subsequent tests may be due as much or more to the lectures as to the program.

The soundness of self-controlled designs is dependent on the appropriateness of the number and timing of measurements. To check retention of learning, should students be tested once? Twice? At what intervals? A program might be considered ineffective just because data were presented too soon for the hoped-for outcomes to occur.

On their own, self-controlled designs are relatively weak. The addition of a control group can strengthen them, as illustrated in Example 2.9.

EXAMPLE 2.9
Combined Self-Control and Concurrent Control Design to Evaluate the Impact of Education and Legislation on Children's Use of Bicycle Helmets

An anonymous questionnaire regarding use of bicycle helmets was sent twice to nearly 3,000 children in three counties. The first mailing took place 3 months before an educational campaign in County 1 and 3 months before the passage of legislation requiring helmets and an education campaign in County 2. The second

mailing took place 9 months after completion of the education and combined education-legislation. Two surveys (9 months apart) were also conducted in County 3, the control. County 3 had neither education nor legislation pertaining to the use of bicycle helmets. The table below summarizes the results.

Percentage of Children
Reporting Use "Always" or "Usually"

	Before Intervention	After Intervention
County 1: Education only	8	13*
County 2: Education and legislation	11	37**
County 3: No intervention	7	8

NOTE: The percentages are small and do not add up to 100% because they represent only the proportion of children answering "always" or "usually." Other responses, such as "rarely," constituted the other choices.

$*p < .01$.

$**p < .0001$ (for more about p values, see **How to Analyze Survey Data**, Vol. 8 in this series).

FINDINGS

The proportion of children who reported that they "always" or "usually" wore a helmet increased significantly ($p < .0001$) from 11% before to 37% in County 2 (education and legislation) and 8% before to 13% ($p < .01$) in County 1 (education only). The increase of 1% in County 3 was not significant.

Education alone and education combined with legislation were relatively effective: either one or both increase the proportion of children reporting helmet use. The education may have taught children to give the socially acceptable responses on the survey, but single education programs alone have not usually encouraged children to give desirable responses to survey questions. The fact that the control group did not improve suggests that Counties 1 and 2's efforts were responsible for the improvements. The addition of the control group adds credibility to the survey results.

HISTORICAL CONTROLS

Surveys that use historical controls rely on data that are available from some other, recorded, source. These data substitute for the data that would come from a concurrent control.

Historical controls include established norms such as scores on standardized tests like the SATs and the MCATs, the results of other surveys conducted with similar groups of people, and vital statistics like birth and death rates. Historical controls are convenient; their main source of bias is the potential lack of comparability between the group on whom the data were originally collected and the group of concern in the survey.

Suppose you were concerned with the proportion of children from birth through age 7 in your county who have a regular source of medical care. You might ask: How do the children in my county, many of whom are poor, compare to other children in the United States with respect to having a regular source of care?

To answer this question, you would follow these four steps:

- Survey the children in your county.

- Find out if comparison data pertaining to U.S. children are available and feasible to obtain.

A good place to find out what is available is to start with city, state, or national health agencies that are responsible for collecting social and health statistics. Another option is to check public and university libraries to find out the type of statistical information they have available to the public and how you get access to it.

- If information is available and feasible to obtain, use it to create a chart to use as a worksheet to record the information you need for your survey.

Suppose you find useful data from the 1988 U.S. National Health Interview Survey of Child Health. Then you can prepare a chart like the following:

	Under Age 1 (%)	1 - 4 Years (%)	5 - 7 Years (%)
All children			
Family income Under $10,000			
$10,000 - $24,999			
$25,000 - $39,999			
$40,000 or more			

- Enter your own survey data into the table and apply the appropriate statistical techniques (for recommended statistical methods to use when comparing percentages, see **How to Analyze Survey Data,** Vol. 8 in this series). Consider the following hypothetical example.

Percentage of Children in Hypothetical County (HC) and the United States (US) With a Regular Source of Medical Care

	Under Age 1 (%)		1 - 4 Years (%)		5 - 7 Years (%)	
	HC	US	HC	US	HC	US
All children	89.9	87.2	92.3	84.5	89.5	90.8
Family income under $10,000	83.7	82.4	86.7	88.3	87.6	88.8
$10,000 - $24,999	95.7	92.7	91.3	92.5	88.5	88.3
$25,000 - $39,999	95.3	91.3	96.1	94.6	90.1	89.4
$40,000 or more	95.3	94.4	97.7	96.5	96.7	94.7

SOURCE: Statistics for the U.S. portion obtained from the 1989 U.S. National Interview Survey of Child Health.

WARNING

 When interpreting the data in the table, remember that they were collected in 1988, and many changes in health care may have occurred since then.

COMBINATIONS

Experimental designs compare one or more groups. The groups may be surveyed before, during, and after any intervention. Variations on these basic elements are possible. A common design in medical studies is the crossover. In the crossover, one group is assigned to the experimental group and the other to the control. After a period of time, the experimental and control groups are withdrawn for a washout period. During this time, no treatment is given. The groups are then given the alternative treatment: The first group now becomes the control and the second group the experimental.

The Solomon four-group design is one that combines the randomized control trial with some groups receiving pre- and postmeasures and some receiving only postmeasures. This is illustrated in Example 2.10.

EXAMPLE 2.10
The Solomon Four-Group Design

Group 1	Premeasure	Program	Postmeasure
Group 2	Premeasure		Postmeasure
Group 3		Program	Postmeasure
Group 4			Postmeasure

In this example, Groups 1 and 3 participated in a new program, but Groups 2 and 4 did not. Suppose the new program aimed to improve employees' awareness of health hazards at their place of work. Using the four-group design (and assuming an effective program), the survey should find the following:

1. In Group 1, awareness on the postmeasure should be greater than on the premeasure.

2. More awareness should be observed in Group 1 than in Group 2.

3. Group 3's postmeasure should show more awareness than Group 2's premeasure.

4. Group 3's postmeasure should show more awareness than Group 4's postmeasure.

This design is a randomized controlled trial, and it incorporates self- and concurrent controls. The use of random and nonrandom assignment in the same study is illustrated in Example 2.11.

EXAMPLE 2.11
Random and Nonrandom
Assignment in a Single Study

Four of 14 eligible participating high schools were grouped into two pairs of demographically similar schools. [This is nonrandom assignment.] A 30% sample of 9th-grade classrooms (16 classrooms totaling 430 students) in the first member of the two pairs of schools was selected at random from the total 9th-grade general education enrollment in these two schools to receive a special AIDS-preventive curriculum in the first semester of the academic year. A 20% random sample of 9th-grade classrooms (10 classrooms totaling 251 students) in the second member of the two pairs served as the comparison or control group and received no formal AIDS curriculum at school that semester. Similarly, a 30% sample of 11th-grade classrooms (13 classrooms totaling 309 students) in the second member of the two pairs of schools was selected at random from the total 11th-grade general education enrollment in these two schools to receive the special prevention curriculum in the second semester of the same academic year, and a 20% random sample of 11th-grade classrooms (13 classrooms totaling 326 students) in the first member of the two pairs served as the comparison or control group. A higher proportion of intervention than comparison students was sampled so that more students would be exposed to the special curriculum. The study design also ensured that none of the four participating high schools would be denied implementation of the special curriculum at Grade 9 or 11.

Descriptions (or Observations)

CROSS-SECTIONAL DESIGNS

Cross-sectional designs result in a portrait of one or many groups at one point in time. These designs are used frequently with standard survey-based measurement (that is, mail and self-administered questionnaires and face-to-face and telephone interviews) and are themselves sometimes called survey designs. Example 2.12 gives six illustrative uses of survey-based measurement and cross-sectional designs.

EXAMPLE 2.12
Surveys and Cross-Sectional Designs

1. A face-to-face interview with refugees to find out their immediate fears and aspirations

2. A questionnaire mailed to consumers to find out perceptions of the quality of the goods and services received when ordering by catalogue

3. A telephone interview with patients to find out what has happened since their last surgery

4. A mailed survey with telephone follow-up to find out if residents are prepared properly for emergencies like fire, flood, and earthquake

5. An interview combined with observations to determine how many children use bicycle helmets over a 2-week period

6. Interviews conducted over 1 month to find out teens' views of the quality of their education in 10 schools

Cross-sectional designs provide a portrait of a group during one time period, now or in the past. Sometimes they rely on more than one type of survey measure. In Example 2.12, mail and telephone surveys are used to find out about residents' emergency preparedness, and observations and interviews are combined for data on helmet use among children.

A cross-sectional design that uses random or probability samples is much more likely to have a study population that is **representative** of the target population. For example, suppose you want to conduct a cross-sectional survey about the joys of jogging as perceived by men over 45 years of age. A random sample of 100 men over 45 who jog three or more times each week is more likely to be representative of jogging men over 45 than a selection of the first 100 jogging men who use the Sports Medicine Clinic. Men who come to the clinic may have more injuries, be more "sportsminded," and have more time to visit clinics than a random sample. These characteristics (and others that cannot be anticipated) can affect the applicability of the survey's results to the target: men over 45 years who jog three or more times each week.

Although the result of a cross-sectional design is a group portrait at one point in time, the survey itself may take several weeks or even months to complete. In Example 2.12, to find out about children's use of helmets takes 2 weeks and to uncover teens' views requires 1 month. The longer periods occur with larger samples and when follow-ups are necessary. With very large groups and long periods of data collection, you must define the period to be covered by the survey. For example, consider conducting a year-long survey of the lifestyles of 10,000 people. Over the 12-month period, the very first people surveyed may lose or gain jobs; this factor may influence their lifestyle. Also, during the year, events such as economic recessions and political upheaval may affect people's lifestyles.

To help ensure a uniform set of responses, follow the example of the 1990 U.S. Census and include a time limit, as illustrated in Example 2.13.

EXAMPLE 2.13
Using Time Limits in Surveys

1990 U.S. Census Question

List on the numbered line below the name of each person living here on *Sunday, April 1*, including all persons staying here who have no other home. If EVERYONE at this address is staying here temporarily and usually lives somewhere else, follow the instructions given below.

COHORT DESIGNS

A cohort is a group of people who have something in common and who remain part of the group over an extended period of time. In public health research, cohort studies are used to investigate the risk factors for a disease and the disease's cause, incidence, natural history, and prognosis. They are prospective designs because the direction of inquiry is forward. Cohort designs require two groups: the cohort and the control. They ask "What will happen?" For example, a cohort design may be used in a study to follow the consequences of living with asthma over a 10-year period. To implement the design, people with and without asthma are surveyed and the results compared. (Without a control group, the design is termed a case series.)

Cohort designs sometimes make use of archival data, that is, data from medical, legal, and financial records. For example, in a study of the consequences of living with asthma (and assuming access to complete and accurate records), you might review the medical records of people who developed asthma 10 years ago and follow their recorded progress over time. Notice that, although you are using historical data (the events already happened and are recorded), the direction of inquiry is forward and thus is a prospective design.

Cohorts come in two varieties. Type A focuses on the same population each time survey data are collected, although the samples may be different. Type B, sometimes called a panel study, focuses on the same sample.

- Type A Cohorts: *Different samples from the same population.* With this type of cohort design, you can conduct five surveys of the lifestyles of the class of 1994 over a period of 10 years. Every 2 years, you will draw a sample of 1994 graduates. In this way, some graduates may be asked to complete all five surveys; others will not be chosen to participate at all. Among the most famous cohort studies is the Framingham, Massachusetts, study of cardiovascular disease begun in 1948 to investigate factors associated with heart disease. Over 6,000 people in Framingham agreed to participate in follow-up interviews and physical examinations every 2 years. Some of the children of the original cohort are also being studied.

- Type B Cohorts: *Same samples.* Type B cohorts or panels are used during elections. Preferences for candidates and views on issues are monitored over time, and the characteristics of supporters and nonsupporters are compared. Type B cohorts are also used to study social, intellectual, and health development in infants and children, as illustrated in Example 2.14.

EXAMPLE 2.14
Cohort Design to Study
Development in Infants and Children

A cohort of infants born in five medical centers was selected for the study if they weighed no more than 2,500 grams (5.5 pounds), were no more than 37 weeks gestational age (the age from conception to birth), and were 40 weeks postconceptual age from January to October. Infants with health or congenital conditions were excluded from the study as were infants whose mothers were under 15 years of age or 25 years or older, could not communicate in English, or were diagnosed with psychiatric illness or alcohol or other drug abuse.

Surveys and assessments were made when each infant was 40 weeks old and 4, 8, 12, 18, 24, 30, and 36 months gestational age. The table below compares the development scores of the infant cohort at 3 years of age.

Characteristic	Intelligence Scores Mean (SD)[a]	Number of Behavior Problems Mean (SD)	Health Rating Index Mean (SD)
Infant gender			
Male	81.0 (17.7)	30.2 (13.5)**	26.7 (5.2)
Female	81.3 (14.6)	25.8 (11.3)	27.7 (4.4)
Birth weight (grams)			
More than 1,500	79.9 (14.9)	29.5 (12.7)	26.4 (5.3)
Less than 1,500	81.6 (16.3)	27.1 (12.3)	27.5 (4.6)
Maternal age (years)			
15 - 17	78.2 (12.0)	29.8 (12.7)	27.0 (4.1)
18 - 19	81.6 (13.3)	29.6 (12.9)	27.4 (5.1)
20 - 24	81.9 (18.0)	26.2 (12.0)	27.3 (4.9)
Family in poverty			
Yes	77.3 (14.2)*	29.5 (13.4)**	27.1 (5.1)
No	87.6 (16.8)	25.0 (10.4)	27.1 (5.1)
Frequent moving			
Yes	80.2 (13.8)	32.0 (13.9)**	27.4 (4.1)
No	81.5 (16.7)	26.3 (11.6)	27.2 (5.0)

a. SD = standard deviation, which is a measure of dispersion or spread around the mean or average.

*$p < .01$—intelligence scores: yes poverty versus no.

**$p < .001$—behavior problems: males versus females; yes poverty versus no; yes moving versus no.

In this cohort of infants, males had significantly more behavior problems than did females. Infants in poverty had significantly lower intelligence scores and more behavior problems. Children who moved frequently had significantly more behavior problems.

Cohort studies sometimes use more than one group. For example, suppose you want to find out if jogging leads to osteo-arthritis, a painful condition that affects weight-bearing joints like the knees and lumbar spine. You might take a group of men over 50 years of age, divide them into a "runners" group and a "nonrunners" group, and collect baseline data. After a period of time, say, 5 years, you can measure if any differences exist in the development or progression of the disorder.

Cohort studies can be expensive because they are longitudinal, requiring measurement at several points in time. They are subject to biases from selection. (Those who are chosen and willing to participate may be inherently different from the remainder of the cohort who are not willing.) Type B cohorts—panels—are also prone to loss of data, with incomplete information collected on important variables or no data collected at all after a certain point in time.

CASE-CONTROL DESIGNS

Case-control designs are retrospective. They are used to help explain why a phenomenon currently exists by comparing two groups, one of which is involved in the phenomenon. For example, a case-control design might be used to help understand the social, demographic, and attitudinal variables that distinguish people with frequent headaches from those without.

The cases in case-control designs are individuals who have been chosen on the basis of some characteristic or outcome (such as frequent headaches). The controls are individuals without the characteristic or outcome. The histories of both groups are analyzed and compared in an attempt to uncover one or more characteristics that are present in the cases but not in the controls.

How can you avoid having one group decidedly different from the other, say, older or smarter? **Matching** is often used in case-control designs to guard against confounding variables. For example, in the case-control study of people with frequent headaches, the two groups selected should be similar in age, education, and duration and severity of the headaches. Example 2.15 illustrates the use of case-control designs in surveys.

EXAMPLE 2.15
A Case-Control Design

The National Teacher Corps was created in 1962 to train highly qualified individuals to enter the teaching profession. For the Corps' 30th anniversary, a study was conducted to find out why some people continued to teach and others had changed careers. People who chose teaching as their career (the cases) were matched to the controls on age, gender, educational background, and other social and demographic variables. The controls consisted of people who taught for 2 or fewer years after completion of the Corps' training program.

Eligible participants were mailed a 100-item questionnaire that asked for information on perceptions of current job satisfaction, willingness to take risks, religious preferences, and living arrangements. The academic records of the two groups were also compared before and after participation in the Corps.

Case-control designs are often used by epidemiologists and other health workers to provide insight into the causes and consequences of disease. These designs are generally less time consuming and expensive than cohorts. Matching is intuitively appealing and feasible.

Case-control designs have their problems, however. First, the groups of cases and controls are selected from two separate populations. Because of this, you cannot be certain that the groups are comparable with respect to extraneous factors like motivation, cultural beliefs, and other expectations (some of which you may not know). Also, the data for case-control designs are historical, often coming from inadequate or incomplete records. Data are sometimes obtained by asking people to recall past events and habits. Memory is often unreliable, however, and this introduces mistakes into the survey's data.

Internal and External Validity

A design with external validity produces results that apply to the survey's target population. An externally valid survey of the preferences of airline passengers over 45 years of age means that the findings apply to all airline passengers of that age.

A design is internally valid if it is free from nonrandom error or bias. A study design must be internally valid to be externally valid and to produce accurate findings. To ensure internal validity, you must be aware of and avoid the common risks given in the following checklist.

Internal Invalidity:
Checklist of Risks to Avoid

✓ Maturation.

Maturation refers to changes within individuals that result from natural, biological, or psychological development. For example, in a 5-year study of a preventive health education program for high school students, the students may mature intellectually and emotionally, and this new maturity may be more important than the program in producing changes in health behavior.

✓ Selection.

Selection refers to how people were chosen for the survey and, if they participate in an experiment, how they were assigned to groups. To avoid selection bias, every eligible person or unit should have an equal, nonzero chance of being included.

✓ History.

Historical events may occur that can bias the study's results. For example, suppose a national campaign has been created to encourage people to make use of preventive health care services. If a change in health insurance laws favoring reimbursement for preventive health care occurs at the same time as the campaign, it may be difficult to separate the effects of the campaign from the effects of increased access to care created by more favorable reimbursement for health care providers.

✓ Instrumentation.

Unless the measures used to collect data are dependable, you cannot be sure that the findings are accurate. For example, in a before-after design, an easier postmeasure than premeasure will erroneously favor an intervention. Also, untrained but lenient observers or test administrators can rule in favor of an intervention's effectiveness, whereas untrained but harsh observers or test administrators can rule against it.

✓ Statistical regression.

Suppose people are chosen for an intervention to foster tolerance. The basis for selection, say, was their extreme views, as measured by a survey. A second administration of the survey (without any intervention) may appear to suggest that the views were somehow softened, but in fact, the results may be a statistical artifact. This is called regression toward the mean and is ubiquitous. Regression effects are the result of factors such as an imperfect test-retest correlation.

✓ Attrition.

Attrition is another word for loss of data such as occurs when participants do not complete all or parts of a survey. People may not complete their surveys because they move away, become ill or bored with participation, and so on. Sometimes, participants who continue to provide complete survey data throughout a long study are different from those who do not.

Risks to external validity are most often the consequence of the way in which participants or respondents are selected and assigned. For example, respondents in an experimental situation may answer questions atypically because they know they are in a special experiment; this is called the "Hawthorne" effect. External validity is also a risk just because respondents are tested, surveyed, or observed. They may become alert to the kinds of behaviors that are expected or favored. Sources of external invalidity to avoid are given in the following checklist.

External Invalidity: Checklist of Risks to Avoid

✓ Reactive effects of testing.

A premeasure can sensitize participants to the aims of an intervention. Suppose two groups of junior high school students are eligible to participate in a program to teach ethics. The first group is surveyed regarding its perspectives on selected ethics issues and then shown a film about young people from different backgrounds faced with ethical dilemmas. The second group of students is just shown the film. It would not be surprising if the first group performed better on a postmeasure if only because the group was sensitized to the purpose of the movie by the questions on the premeasure.

✓ **Interactive effects of selection.**

This occurs when an intervention and the participants are a unique mixture: one that may not be found elsewhere. Suppose a school volunteers to participate in an experimental program to improve the quality of students' leisure time activities. The characteristics of the school (some of which may be related to the fact that it volunteered for the experiment) may interact with the program so that the two together are unique; the particular blend of school and intervention can limit the applicability of the findings.

✓ **Reactive effects of innovation.**

Sometimes, the environment of an experiment is so artificial that all who participate are aware that something special is going on and behave uncharacteristically.

✓ **Multiple program interference.**

It is sometimes difficult to isolate the effects of an experimental intervention because of the possibility that participants are in other complementary activities or programs.

Example 2.16 illustrates how internal and external validity are affected in two different designs.

EXAMPLE 2.16
How the Choice of Design May
Affect Internal and External Validity

Concurrent Controls Without Random Assignment

Description: The Food Allergy Mediation Alliance (FAMA) is a year-long program for people with food allergies. Eligible people can enroll in one of two variations of the program. To find out if participants are satisfied with the quality of the program, both groups complete an in-depth questionnaire at the end of the year, and the results are compared.

Comment: The internal validity is potentially marred by the fact that the participants in the groups may be different from one another at the beginning of the program. More severely allergic persons may choose one program over the other, for example. Also, because of initial differences, the attrition rate may be affected. The failure to create randomly constituted groups will jeopardize the study's external validity by the interactive effects of selection.

Concurrent Controls With Randomization

Description: The Make-A-Wish Trust commissioned an evaluation of three different interventions for visually impaired children. Eligible children were randomly assigned to one of the three interventions, baseline data were collected, and a 3-year investigation was made of effectiveness and efficiency. At the end of the 3 years, the children were examined to determine their functioning on a number of variables including school performance and behavior at home and at school. The children were also interviewed extensively throughout the study. The results of the examinations and interviews were compared with those obtained from a study of visually impaired children who had participated in a similar experiment in another part of the country.

Comment: This design is internally valid. Because children were randomly assigned to each intervention, any sources of change that might compete with the intervention's impact will affect all three groups equally. To improve external validity, the findings from a study of other children will be compared with those from the Make-A-Wish Trust. This additional comparison does not guarantee that the results will hold for a third group of children. Another consideration is that school administrators and staff may not spend as much money as usual because they know the study involves studying efficiency (reactive effects of innovation). Finally, we do not know if and how baseline data collection affected children's performance and interviews (interaction between testing and the intervention).

Eight Commonly Used Study Designs

Design	Benefits	Risks	Potential for Bias or Invalidity
Concurrent controls and random assignment (randomized controlled or control trial; true experiment)	If properly conducted, can establish the extent to which a program caused its outcomes	Proper implementation requires resources and methodologic expertise	*Internal validity:* Excellent *External validity:* If a premeasure is given, possibility of reactive effects of testing; reactive effects of innovation
Concurrent controls without randomization (quasi-experimental)	Easier to implement than a randomized control trial	A wide range of potential biases may occur because, without an equal chance of selection, participants in the program may be systematically different from those in the control group	*Internal validity:* Selection, attrition, cannot be sure about maturation *External validity:* Interactive effects of selection
Self-controls (pretest-posttest)	Relatively easy to implement logistically Provides data on change	Must be certain that measurements are appropriately timed Without a control group, you cannot tell if effects are also present in other groups	*Internal validity:* Maturation, history, instrumentation, and interaction of selection with other factors; regression a possibility *External validity:* Interaction of selection, reactive effects of testing, and possibly reactive effects of innovation

→

Design	Benefits	Risks	Potential for Bias or Invalidity
Historical controls	Easy to implement; unobtrusive	Must make sure that "normative" comparison data are applicable to participants	*Internal validity:* Selection, attrition, interaction of selection with other factors; cannot be sure about maturation *External validity:* Interactive effects of selection
Solomon four-group	Rigorous design that permits inferences about causes Guards against the effects of the premeasure on subsequent performance	Need to have enough participants to constitute four groups Expensive to implement	*Internal validity:* Excellent *External validity:* Possibility of interaction of selection and reactive effects of innovation
Cross-sectional	Provides baseline information on survey participants and descriptive information about the intervention	Offers a picture of participants and program at one point in time	*Internal validity:* If survey is lengthy, then history and maturation; selection, attrition *External validity:* Only if sample is representative are findings applicable to population

Design	Benefits	Risks	Potential for Bias or Invalidity
Cohort	Provides longitudinal or follow-up information	Can be expensive because they are relatively long-term studies Participants who are available over time may differ in important ways from those who are not	*Internal validity:* Maturation, history, instrumentation, and interaction of selection with other factors; regression a possibility *External validity:* Interaction of selection and the intervention; reactive effects of testing and possibly reaction to innovation
Case-control	Can provide insights into the causes and consequences of disease Generally less time-consuming and expensive than cohorts	The compared groups of cases and controls are selected from two separate populations and you cannot be certain that the groups are comparable with respect to extraneous factors (some of which you may not know) Data often come from records, which may be inadequate or incomplete	*Internal validity:* Selection, attrition, interaction of selection with other factors; cannot be sure about maturation *External validity:* Interactive effects of selection and intervention

Exercises

1. A team of experts spent 5 days interviewing all part-time employees. Which of the following study designs is being used? *Circle one choice.*

Cross-sectional	1
Self-control	2
Concurrent controls without randomization	3
Historical controls	4

2. The goals and aspirations of the 1990 graduates of the three major types of high schools (arts and sciences, vocational, and technical) are followed over 10 years. Each year, the 1990 graduates are interviewed and filmed. Which of the following study designs is being used? *Circle one choice.*

Case-control	1
Cohort	2
Self-control	3
Quasi-experiment	4

3. What are the threats to internal and external validity of these two survey designs?

   a. The ABC Sales Company experimented with a program to help minorities and women get and keep higher-paying jobs. Human resources staff interviewed all employees and examined records to collect data on the program's effectiveness.

   b. An evaluation of three 1-month rehabilitation programs for patients with heart disease was conducted. Patients were free to select the program of their choice. The evaluation team collected information on whether patients' knowledge of their condition and self-confidence had improved. To answer the question, patients in each program were surveyed before and after program participation.

ANSWERS

1. Cross-sectional

2. Cohort

3. a: Internal validity may be affected by historical events, such as new legislation, that may occur at the same time as the program; these events may be more influential than the program. Also, employees may change job ranks naturally over time. Finally, the people who remain employed and in the program may be inherently different (e.g., more skilled) from others who are fired or move away. External validity may be influenced by the reactive effects of innovation.

   b: Selection is a possible risk to internal validity because participants in the two groups may have been different from one another at the beginning of the program. For example, healthier people may choose one program over the other. Also, attrition may be different between the two groups. The external validity is limited by a number of factors including the reactive effects of innovation, interactive effects of selection, and possibly multiple program interference.

Suggested Readings

Brett, A., & Grodin, M. (1991). Ethical aspects of human experimentation in health services research. *Journal of the American Medical Association, 265,* 1854-1857.

This article is an extremely important one because of its implications for experimental designs. The "participants" in experiments and their surveys are human, so the requirements of informed consent apply as do concepts like respect for privacy.

Campbell, D. T., & Stanley, J. C. (1963). *Experimental and quasi-experimental designs for research.* Chicago: Rand McNally.

The classic book on differing research designs. "Threats" to internal and external validity are described in detail. Issues pertaining to generalizability and how to get at "truth" are important reading.

Dawson-Saunders, B., & Trapp, R. G. (1990). *Basic and clinical bio-statistics.* East Norwalk, CT: Appleton & Lange.

Chapter 2 discusses study designs in medical research and their advantages and disadvantages. Examples are given of the use of the designs.

Fink, A. (1993). *Evaluation fundamentals: Guiding health programs, research, and policy.* Newbury Park, CA: Sage.

Chapter 3 covers the range of designs that are useful in program evaluations. The Evaluation Design Report is discussed as are the roles of independent variables in design and sampling.

Kosecoff, J., & Fink, A. (1982). *Evaluation basics.* Beverly Hills, CA: Sage.

Chapter 4 discusses alternative designs and threats to internal and external validity.

About the Author

ARLENE FINK, PhD, is Professor of Medicine and Public Health at the University of California, Los Angeles. She is on the Policy Advisory Board of UCLA's Robert Wood Johnson Clinical Scholars Program, a health research scientist at the Veterans Administration Medical Center in Sepulveda, California, and president of Arlene Fink Associates. She has conducted evaluations throughout the United States and abroad and has trained thousands of health professionals, social scientists, and educators in program evaluation. Her published works include nearly 100 monographs and articles on evaluation methods and research. She is coauthor of *How to Conduct Surveys* and author of *Evaluation Fundamentals: Guiding Health Programs, Research, and Policy* and *Evaluation for Education and Psychology.*

73